Nanotechnology

Rebecca L. Johnson

LERNER PUBLICATIONS COMPANY
MINNEAPOLIS

Lerner Publications Company
A division of Lerner Publishing Group
241 First Avenue North
Minneapolis, MN 55401 U.S.A.

Website address: www.lernerbooks.com

Library of Congress Cataloging-in-Publication Data

Johnson, Rebecca L.
        Nanotechnology / by Rebecca L. Johnson.
            p.   cm. — (Cool science)
        Includes bibliographical references and index.
        ISBN-13: 978–0–8225–2111–2 (lib. bdg. : alk. paper)
        ISBN-10: 0–8225–2111–3 (lib. bdg. : alk. paper)
        1. Nanotechnology—Juvenile literature. I. Title. II. Series.
    T174.7.J6 2006
    620'.5—dc22   2005008791

Manufactured in the United States of America
1 2 3 4 5 6 – BP – 11 10 09 08 07 06

Table of Contents

Introduction

Imagine you and your older sister are heading to the beach. The time: today. You're driving along in the family car. You're eating a chocolate ice-cream cone.

Your sister pulls into a parking space. But she doesn't brake quite hard enough. BAM! The car's front bumper hits the guard rail. The jolt knocks your ice cream into your lap. The two of you jump out to see what happened. Amazingly, the bumper isn't dented or scratched. Your sister breathes a sigh of relief. You look down at your shorts. They are covered with drops of melted ice cream. With one swipe, you brush the droplets off. No stain to explain.

IT'S A FACT!

Each year there are more than 6 million car accidents in the United States. Car makers and the government spend millions of dollars researching new ways to make cars stronger, safer, and easier to repair.

"Here, put this on your nose," your sister says as you walk toward the beach. She tosses you a tube of zinc oxide sunscreen cream. You hate that white stuff on your nose. But wait—this kind is clear. Cool!

Now imagine another day—twenty years from now. You have kids of your own, and you're driving to the beach. As you pull into the parking lot, the sunlight glints off your clean windshield. It's always clean—it cleans itself. You swing into a

While you may enjoy a day at the beach, you might hate that white, pasty zinc oxide on your nose. Thanks to nanotechnology, the sunblocker is now clear.

parking space. You don't worry about hitting the guard rail. An onboard, sugar-cube-sized computer guides your car into place.

"Can I have a green towel?" asks one of your kids. You grab a red towel and push a little pad in one corner. Instantly, the red towel turns green. You dab sunscreen on her arm. It will soon spread all over her skin by itself. And it will protect her from germs as well as from the sun. As your kids run off toward the waves, you take your laptop out of your pocket and unfold it. You might as well check your e-mail before you have a swim.

Indestructible bumpers? Stainless clothes? Thanks to nanotechnology, these things are a reality today. And in the not-too-distant future, nanotechnology will be giving the world self-cleaning windows, fabrics that change color, and much, much more.

So what is nanotechnology? It's something very small that is going to affect your life in a big way.

chapter 1

It's a Small, Small World

Nanotechnology is a new scientific field that involves moving individual atoms and molecules around to create new things on an ultra-small scale. Some of these things are never-seen-before materials with remarkable properties. Others are tiny "machines"—smaller than microscopic viruses—that can do specific jobs.

Nanotechnology is a whole new way of building things. Take a look around. Almost every manufactured thing you see—tables, computers, shoes, books—has been made from preexisting materials such as wood, stone, cotton, metal, leather, and plastic. These materials have been cut, shaped, ground down, woven, and formed into these objects.

Nanotechnology works the other way around. It doesn't start with big things and whittle them down. It builds things from the bottom up, atom by atom and molecule by molecule.

Basic Building Blocks

Atoms and molecules are the building blocks of nanotechnology. They are also the building blocks of all matter, from air and rocks and water to plants and animals and people. Your body is made up of billions and billions of atoms.

You can think of an atom as the smallest complete unit of matter. But single atoms are pretty rare in nature. Atoms typically join together to form molecules. Some molecules contain all the same kind of atom. Many other molecules are made up of different kinds of atoms.

Bonded Together

If an atom were a grape, a molecule would be a cluster of grapes. Molecules exist as small clusters, huge clusters, and everything in between. Atoms tend to stay clustered together in molecules because of bonds. Bonds are electrical forces (some strong, some weak) that hold atoms—and molecules—together. Bonds play a big role in how atoms and molecules cluster and behave.

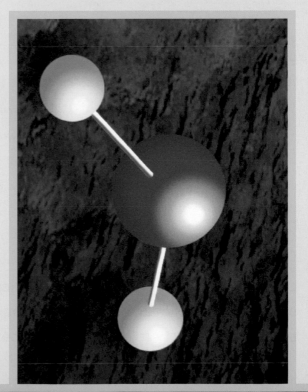

Water, or H2O, is one of the simplest-known molecules. A water molecule is two hydrogen atoms (green) bonded to one oxygen atom (red).

An artist created this image of human hands working with molecules to illustrate the science of nanotechnology. Nanotechnology scientists study and work with arranging atoms and molecules to create new materials and structures.

All-Important Arrangements

It's how atoms and molecules are arranged that gives different kinds of matter different properties. Take coal and diamonds. Both these substances are made up of carbon atoms. Coal is black and soft, and it burns. Diamonds are clear and one of the hardest materials known. The difference between coal and diamonds depends on how their carbon atoms are arranged.

The arrangement of atoms and molecules in a substance determines its characteristics. So it makes sense that rearranging those atoms and molecules will change the substance's characteristics. Imagine being able to control how atoms and molecules are put together. If you could do that, you could also control—very precisely—the characteristics of whatever you were making. That, in a nutshell, is a big part of what nanotechnology is all about.

Measuring on a Nanoscale

Nanotechnology is a field where things are measured in nanometers. In science, the prefix *nano-* means 1 billionth of something. So a nanometer (nm) is 1 billionth of a meter.

How small is that? A human hair is about 40,000 nanometers thick. A single red blood cell measures about 7,500 nanometers across. Here's another way to visualize how small a nanometer is: Hold a meterstick or a yardstick out in front of you. Now imagine stretching that stick from Los Angeles to New York City. At that scale, a nanometer would be about the size of a ladybug!

Nano Measurements

Nano- comes from the Greek word *nanos*, which means "midget" or "dwarf." The name *nanotechnology* was coined in 1974 by Norio Taniguchi, a scientist working at

the University of Tokyo in Japan. In nanotechnology, this prefix is used a lot to describe small structures such as nanoparticles, nanodevices, or anything else measured on the nanoscale.

The nanoscale measures unbelievably small objects. Human hairs (left) are quite large on the nanoscale, each measuring about 40,000 nanometers thick. Many objects scientists measure on the nanoscale are much, much smaller—undetectable to the human eye.

Small Stuff, Big Deal

Nanotechnology deals with structures, devices, and systems that are just 1 to 100 nanometers in size. That's much, much smaller than anything you can see with the naked eye. In fact, you can only see objects on the nanoscale with the newest, most powerful microscopes.

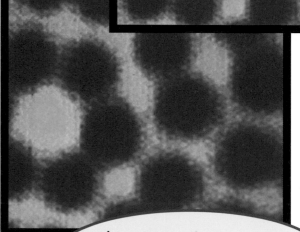

So why are these incredibly small things so important? Why is nanotechnology making the news almost every day? Imagine materials that are hundreds of times stronger than steel but weigh only a fraction as much. Think of computer chips that store trillions of bits of information but are no bigger than the head of a pin. Picture tiny devices that move through your bloodstream attacking germs. Or miniscule machines that assemble molecules to build big, complex objects—all by themselves.

A scientist took this picture of silicon atoms using a powerful, modern microscope.

From Science Fiction to Science Fact

Does all that sound like science fiction? Fifty years ago, most people would have dismissed nanotechnology as just that. But what once seemed like fiction is starting to become reality.

Some people predict that as scientists get better at manipulating atoms and molecules—at building things from the bottom up—the results will change everything from clothes, cars, and construction materials to medicine, electronics, and space exploration. Nanotechnology has the potential to revolutionize the way we live. That revolution may bring us new problems too. But before we look at where nanotechnology might take us, let's see how it began.

FUN FACT!

Nanotechnology is a combination of sciences. Just as engineers design bridges and buildings, nanotechnologists design and build nanostructures. They also use molecular chemistry (how atoms and molecules work) and biochemistry (the chemical processes in living organisms) in their work.

Engines of Creation

In 1986, K. Eric Drexler wrote a book called *Engines of Creation*. In the book, Drexler analyzed the potential power of nanotechnology and predicted how it would change people's lives. The book created a lot of controversy and made nanotechnology a household word. It also got many scientists and companies interested in doing nanoscale research. Drexler went on to establish the Foresight Institute, a non-profit educational organization that aims to help society prepare for new technological revolutions.

Dr. K. Eric Drexler peers through a large-scale model of a special carbon molecule. Drexler has been a leader in the development of nanotechnology.

chapter 2

New Tools, New Technology

In 1981, physicists Gerd Binnig and Heinrich Rohrer, working at a research laboratory near Zurich, Switzerland, invented a new kind of microscope. They called it a scanning tunneling microscope (STM). It offered scientists a new view of matter.

By moving an extremely sharp probe over a tiny sample of a metal material, someone using an STM can produce an image of individual atoms on the material's surface. The image is like a little contour map, with dips and bumps that reveal the atoms' shape.

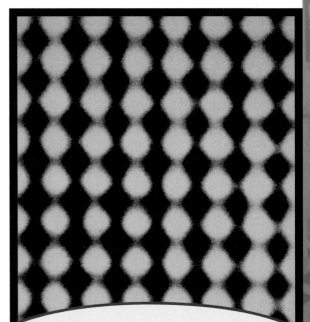

An STM image of atoms (*gold spheres*) forming gold. With the STM, scientists could view matter at its basic level.

The STM was an amazing break-through. For the first time in the history of science, it was possible to see atoms and molecules! Then, just five years later, Binnig and his coworkers invented the atomic force microscope (AFM). It also produces images of atoms and molecules, but it works with any substance, not just metals.

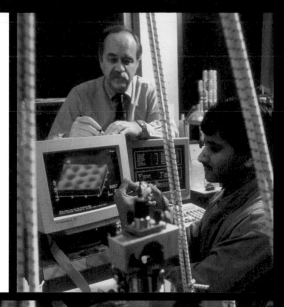

These new microscopes allowed scientists to do more than just look, however. They discovered that they could actually move atoms around using the micro-scopes' finely tipped probes.

Nanoscientists work with an AFM *(center)* to observe and photograph atoms and molecules. AFMs use electromagnetism *(magnetic energy)* to see and move atoms.

Richard Feynman

In 1959, physicist Richard Feynman was speaking at a meeting of the American Physical Society. A brilliant scientist, Feynman proposed revolutionary ideas about reducing the size of (miniaturizing) circuits and machines. Although he didn't know how it would happen, Feynman was convinced that one day it would become possible to manipulate atoms and molecules "on a small scale." Thirty years later, other scientists proved he'd been right. In some ways, Feynman can be considered the father of nanotechnology.

In November 1989, Eigler and Schweitzer arranged thirty-five xenon atoms to spell out the IBM company's logo (above). The special logo could fit in the period at the end of this sentence more than 300 million times.

In 1989, California scientists Donald Eigler and Erhard Schweizer used an STM to painstakingly move xenon gas atoms—one at a time—to spell out the name of the company they worked for: IBM. They created the world's smallest logo, just a few nanometers in size!

As other scientists explored the power of STMs and AFMs, they learned how to add atoms, one at a time, to a growing molecule. Although building molecules this way was slow and tedious, it was a start. And it got a lot of people thinking that maybe the idea of nanotechnology wasn't so farfetched after all.

Enter Buckyballs

Nanotechnology got another boost in 1985. A group of chemists working at Rice University in Texas discovered the first potential nanomaterial. Up until then, the chemical element carbon was only known to exist in two forms: diamond and graphite (the basic substance in coal and pencil lead). While examining soot produced during a laboratory experiment, Robert Curl, Harold Kroto, and Richard Smalley discovered tiny balls of carbon in the soot. The carbon balls were just a few nanometers in diameter.

Smalley and the others had discovered an entirely new form of carbon. They called it buckminsterfullerene, or fullerene for short. Because of the round shape of fullerene molecules, people started calling them buckyballs.

A great deal of excitement surrounded the discovery of buckyballs. Could these tiny little spheres be used for building nanostructures? Could they be used like tiny ball bearings in nanomachines?

Buckyballs' Namesake

A molecule of fullerene is made up of sixty carbon atoms bonded together in a many-sided structure that looks something like a soccer ball. This new form of carbon was named after U.S. architect Richard Buckminster Fuller (1895–1983) because of its resemblance to geodesic domes, building structures that Fuller invented.

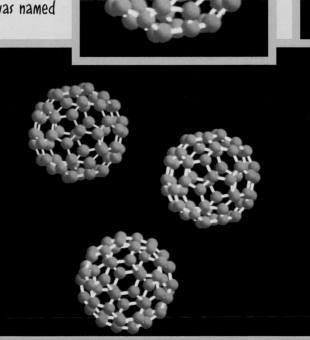

Buckyballs, or buckminsterfullerene, molecules (right). Buckyballs may hold part of the answer to building nanomachines and other structures.

Carbon Nanotubes

While some scientists were studying buckyballs, Japanese physicist Sumio Iijima was working in his lab one day in 1991. Under an electron microscope, he noticed some nano-sized "threads" in a smear of soot. The threads turned out to be extremely thin tubes of pure carbon. These carbon tubes were just a few nanometers in diameter but many nanometers long.

A carbon nanotube (*blue*) stretches across two pieces of platinum metal (*golden*). This nanotube is 10 atoms wide, and it can carry an electrical current, making it the world's smallest wire to date.

Carbon nanotubes are light and flexible. But they are incredibly strong for their size. They are possibly the strongest material known. Carbon nanotubes also have other interesting properties. For instance, heat and electricity move easily through them.

Carbon nanotubes, rather than buckyballs, turned out to be nanotechnology's first building blocks. (Buckyballs weren't forgotten, though.) And just as you might play around with Legos to see what you could build, scientists in laboratories all over the world began experimenting with these tiny carbon tubes to learn more about them and how they might be used to create nanostructures.

FUN FACT!

Nanotechnology research labs must include a "clean room." Because researchers are working with extremely sensitive equipment, the lab environment must be carefully controlled. In a clean room, the air is continuously filtered to remove even the tiniest bits of dust. Temperature and humidity (the amount of dampness in the air) are kept at exact levels. And clean rooms are built to minimize vibrations from car or people traffic. Researchers also often wear masks and special ultraclean clothing.

chapter 3

Learning to Use Nanomaterials

For something so small and seemingly simple, carbon nanotubes are pretty amazing things. Although you may not know it, they've already had an impact on our lives.

Many plastics shatter when hit hard. One of the first practical applications that researchers found for carbon nanotubes was to mix them into plastics. The result was lightweight, rustproof car bumpers that take a beating and come out without a scratch or dent. Paint also sticks better to car parts that contain these nanomaterials.

Futuristic Fabrics

What do you get when you mix carbon nanotubes and fabrics? Stainless pants! That's what University of California, Berkeley, chemical engineer David Sloane discovered when he added tiny carbon nanotubes to such fabrics as wool and cotton. The nanotubes bond to the

A sharp ice pick cannot puncture this material of plastic and carbon nanotubes developed for the U.S. Army. The fabric makes the best body armor to date.

fabric's fibers. They create a "nanobarrier" between the fabric and its surroundings. Spilled liquids simply bead up on the treated cloth and can be brushed off like lint.

Other researchers have created a new synthetic fiber that is formed from carbon nanotubes and plastic. It's many times stronger than Kevlar. That's the tough stuff currently used to make bulletproof vests. By weaving the new fiber into fabric, researchers hope to make clothing that's lightweight but nearly indestructible.

Nanowhiskers

Stainless pants, shorts, skirts, and jeans are as close as your nearest department store. But you can't see or even feel the carbon nanotubes that cover the surface of the fabric. They do their job invisibly. David Sloane calls the short nanotubes used in stainless fabrics "nanowhiskers." That's because under a microscope, the treated fabric looks like it needs a shave!

Other Nanomaterials

When it comes to nanomaterials, carbon nanotubes are just the beginning. Do you play tennis? Then be on the lookout for nanotech tennis balls. These new balls keep their bounce twice as long as ordinary tennis balls. That's because they are lined on the inside with a 1-nanometer layer of special clay. This nanolayer locks the air inside and doubles the life of the ball. Combine these nano-enhanced tennis balls with a super strong, ultralightweight tennis racket (made by adding carbon nanotubes to the frame), and you could really improve your tennis game!

A nanolayer added to the lining of the DC2 tennis ball creates a strong seal, keeping air inside it twice as long as other tennis balls. Nanotubes mixed with other materials in this racket's frame make it ultralight and superstrong.

While you're out on the tennis court, don't forget the sunscreen. But the days of putting ugly white goop on your nose are gone.

Nanotechnologists have figured out how to break down zinc oxide (a sub-stance that protects skin against sun-burn) into super-small nanoparticles. Added to sunscreen cream, the parti-cles filter out the sun's harmful rays. But the cream looks clear because the particles are so tiny they're invisible to the naked eye.

FUN FACT!

Ultraviolet (UV) light causes sunburn, and it also damages other things. But clear nanoparticles of zinc oxide offer protection. They can be made into a UV-filter coating for glass or plastic, on windows or sunglasses. The nanoparticles can be mixed into fiberglass and paint to prevent sun damage to cars, boats, and buildings.

The List Goes On

Perhaps tennis isn't your sport. How about skiing or snowboarding? You'll find nanotechnology on the slopes too.

Some manufacturers are coating the bottom of skis and snowboards with nanoparticles of wax. The coating is just a few atoms thick. But it bonds tightly, so it lasts far longer than regular wax.

Nanodolls

Even toys have become a part of the nanotechnology revolution. Nanocrystals that change shape when exposed to an electric current are finding their way into dolls. Flip a switch, and the doll smiles and frowns. The doll's "nanomuscles" contract like real muscles—but with 1,000 times the strength!

Baby Bright Eyes has nanomuscles controlling her eyes, resulting in eye movement that is nearly human.

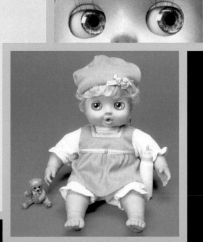

There's another plus. The nanoparticles are water-repellent. They prevent ice from building up on skis and boards, so you get a faster ride!

If you take a tumble and scrape some skin, don't worry. Thanks to nanotechnology, doctors and nurses have some new tools in their medical kits. They might cover your wound with a bandage that's coated with bacteria-killing nanocrystals. You can't see the crystals. But they'll kill any germs hanging around in as little as 30 minutes.

The list of new products developed through nanotechnology research goes on and on. Glass companies are making self-cleaning windows. The glass is coated with nanoparticles that prevent dirt from sticking.

Rainwater blurs a regular window (left panes). But the sides treated with a nanolayer of protection remain clear (right panes). The nanosurface on this window also helps clean it. When sunlight hits the nanolayer, a chemical reaction occurs, dissolving dirt.

Many cosmetics, hair condition-ers, and face creams contain nanoparticles that improve these products. Drug companies are exploring ways to add nanoparti-cles of certain medicines to skin lotions. People would just rub the lotion on their skin, and the medicine would be instantly ab-sorbed into the body.

Just about everywhere you look, you'll find nanotechnology in action. But what about the future?

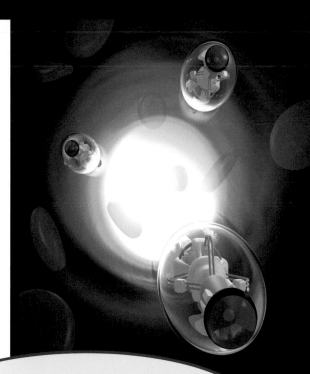

An artist envisions how very small machines called nanobots would look in the bloodstream. Still a dream, nanobots are one possible medical invention from nanotechnology.

chapter 4

What's in the Nanofuture?

Even by themselves, nanomaterials are pretty cool. But nanotechnology has really just taken its first baby steps. Be prepared for giant strides in the not-too-distant future.

As tools and technologies improve, scientists expect to be able to do more than just mix up nanoparticles or coat things with them. They hope to assemble complex molecules to create microscopic nanodevices that will carry out specific tasks. One area where nanotechnology is expected to have a big impact is medicine.

FUN FACT!

In 2001, U.S. president Bill Clinton established the National Nanotechnology Initiative. The program supports research in nanotechnology. The main goal is to develop new nanomaterials and to create new nanoscale processes and devices. Other goals include educating scientists for nanotechnology research.

Actor-scientists in the 1966 film *Fantastic Voyage* are miniaturized to fit inside their nanosubmarine. While such technology remains fiction, nanotechnologists are developing nanotools that one day may be used inside the human body.

Back in the 1960s, the science fiction movie *Fantastic Voyage* wowed audiences across the country. The plot? A team of doctors—along with their high-tech submarine—were miniaturized by a mysterious scientific process. Their job was to travel through the bloodstream of an injured man and remove a blood clot from his brain.

Playing Tag

Your doctor won't be shrinking to enter your bloodstream anytime soon. But it's very likely doctors one day will be using some nanotech tools currently being developed to detect and treat diseases.

Take quantum dots, for example. These are very small nanocrystals that glow in bright neon colors when exposed to ultraviolet light. Researchers are using quantum dots to find and mark certain kinds of cells, such as cancer cells, in living things (frogs and mice, so far).

When the dots are injected, they travel around the body, bumping into cells. Cancer cells tend to gobble them up. In doing so, the cancer cells are "tagged." They glow—brightly enough to be seen through skin if they are close to the body's surface. Researchers follow the glow to find the cancer cells and figure out if the disease is spreading and how fast.

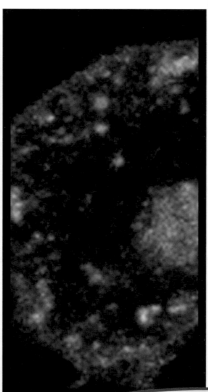 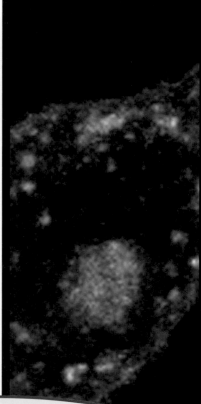

Quantum dots (small, red spheres) in cells help scientists and doctors find and tag (label) damaged cells in the body. These tiny, human-made dots can also carry medicine directly to cells that need it.

A computer-generated model of a medicine-delivering nanosphere.

Nanospheres are made from many materials, including gold, silver, glass, and plastic. Like quantum dots, these spheres can be coated or filled with medicines, dyes, and other substances to probe, heal, and label.

Tiny Trackers

In nanotechnology labs across the United States, researchers are developing all sorts of nanosensors and nanoprobes. They hope to use these minute sensors to detect different kinds of diseases.

For example, tiny nanospheres made of gold and other substances may soon be tracking down diseases in people. One technique being developed uses nanospheres coated with antibodies. Antibodies are infection-fighting molecules produced in your blood when you get sick. Antibody-coated nanospheres injected into a person's bloodstream would latch on to infection-causing cells. In so doing, they'd help doctors detect diseases and pinpoint infections.

As technology improves, nanotechnologists envision more complex sensors. Imagine brushing your teeth with a toothbrush equipped with clusters of nanosensors. They'll test for infections in your body every time you brush your teeth!

Drug Deliveries

Other tools in the nanomedicine chest include tiny packaging systems that would deliver drugs to specific places in a person's body. It's here that buckyballs may prove to be useful.

Researchers are experimenting with buckyballs that can be filled with cancer drugs. Cancer drugs are designed to kill cancer cells. But some are so strong that they kill healthy cells too. Buckyballs filled with cancer drugs could solve this problem. The little nanospheres would be coated with molecules that attach only to cancer cells. After attaching to their targets, the buckyballs would open, releasing their contents and killing the cancer cells. Healthy cells nearby, however, would not be harmed. Other diseases, such as AIDS, might also be treated this way.

Mini Motors

In *Fantastic Voyage*, the miniaturized doctors eventually reach the brain and destroy the life-threatening blood clot. Nanotechnologists hope some day to equip doctors with nanodevices that can travel anywhere inside your body to carry out similar search-and-destroy missions. They also foresee creating nanomachines that will fix body structures that need repairs.

Such nanodevices aren't a reality yet. But scientists are working on building the parts needed to construct them. In 2003, a team of researchers from Purdue University in Indiana built a powerful nanoscale motor from RNA and DNA—molecules that occur naturally in every living thing. The molecular motor is made up of a six-sided "gear" that can turn on a little "shaft." The entire structure is about 1/3000th the width of a human hair!

RNA and DNA

RNA (ribonucleic acid) and DNA (deoxyribonucleic acid) are basic molecules in living things. DNA carries information about all an organism's inherited traits—size, sex, eye color, and other characteristics. RNA works to turn the information stored in DNA into proteins, which are the building blocks of cells. Many nanotechnologists think RNA and DNA will be key parts for building nanomachines.

The scientists can make the motor run by adding a natural fuel called ATP. That's the same energy molecule that powers muscle movements and many other processes in your body. The motor has already been used to destroy a virus inside a living cell. One day, it may power machines that remove fat deposits from inside blood vessels, replace faulty genes in cells, and maybe even clean the plaque off your teeth!

RNA

RNA

RNA

DNA

RNA

The six-bladed DNA-packaging motor developed by scientists at Purdue University. ATP, a form of energy, causes a chemical reaction in the motor's DNA. The energy from this reaction moves outward to the RNA blades, causing them to move the motor in a circular motion.

RNA

Replacement Parts

If you've ever broken a bone, you know how long it can take to heal. Nanotechnologists are designing nanocrystals and other nanomaterials that can mix with the body's own cells to help regrow broken bones in far less time than it takes naturally. Someday, similar techniques may help doctors rebuild other body organs using nanomaterial frameworks on which living cells can grow.

Super-Small Computers

Nanotechnology is expected to have a huge impact in computer technology. Every year, computers get faster and smaller. The material that has made this possible so far is silicon. The "brain" of a computer is built around silicon chips. These chips are packed with tiny circuits (electrical pathways) that are involved in the computer's operation.

Silicon chips begin as silicon crystals. Unwanted material is carefully carved away to create the necessary circuits. But there are size limits to making computer chips this way. At super-small sizes, circuits become packed together too tightly for the chips to work properly.

FUN FACT!

Computer size depends mainly on the size of processing chips and circuitry. Once filling entire rooms, computers now fit on desktops or in the hand. Nanotechnology holds the promise of even smaller, faster computers.

Nanotechnology promises to revolutionize computers. Nanocomputers of the future will use nanochips built molecule by molecule, from the bottom up. There will be no waste, and the circuits will be perfect. And they will be very, very small. So small that you may be doing your college homework on a computer with a hard drive the size of a postage stamp. It may be

The white globs on this biochip (*left*) are atoms. The atoms represent data (information) just like the white pits on this CD-ROM (*above*). The biochip's advantage is that it is thousands of times smaller than a CD and can store far more information.

thousands, even millions, of times faster than any computer you've worked on before. By adding nanomaterials to computer keyboards and screens, your future computer may also be flexible enough to fold up and tuck into your pocket.

There's a long way to go before nanocomputers become a reality. But in 2001, scientists built the first molecule-sized circuit. They are tinkering with nanotubes and nanowires. Every year brings breakthroughs in constructing the tiny components that may one day be put together to create the first nanocomputer.

Cool Stuff!

Nanotechnology may change your life in other ways. New nanomaterials may find their way into just about everything, from cars and planes to the products on grocery store shelves.

How many things do you use that run on batteries? CD players? Toys? Radios? Flashlights? Cameras? Computer games? Then you know how annoyingly fast most batteries run out of power. Because of their electronic properties, carbon nanotubes added to batteries may help them last longer. What's more, nanotech batteries will probably be much smaller than regular batteries—and they'll bend!

Expect to see new gadgets in cars, from sensors that help people park in tight spaces to windshields that repair themselves if they're cracked. New nanomaterials will make jet airplanes stronger and lighter. The same is true for spacecraft. Nanomaterials will help reduce the size and weight of spacecraft. They'll also reduce the weight of things we want to transport into space or send to another planet.

Nanotechnology may be part of almost everything we manufacture in the coming years. But it is already at work in many products, including this contact lens. A nanolayer on the lens delivers medicine to an infected eye.

Down on earth, it's likely that we'll have new kinds of construction materials. Buildings may finally be made earthquake-proof, because nanomaterials will absorb shocks and prevent the structures from being shaken apart.

Thanks to other kinds of nanomaterials, the outsides of buildings could change color to absorb or release heat. This would save energy by

An Elevator to Outer Space?

NASA (National Aeronautics and Space Administration) and the U.S. Air Force have been pondering the idea of building an elevator into space for many years. If such a thing could be built, it certainly would be cheaper than rockets for sending people and objects into space. The problem has always been finding materials that were strong enough, yet lightweight enough, to stretch miles out from the earth's surface. The answer may be carbon nanotubes. At least one scientist has suggested creating an unbreakable ribbon cable made of carbon nanotubes to do the job. There are still lots of problems to solve, though, before an elevator into space becomes a reality.

An artist's view of what a nanoconstructed space elevator might look like

reducing the fuel and electricity needed to keep them warm or cool. Better still, nanotechnology may produce tiny solar cells that convert sunlight directly into electricity. Add these to paint that is sprayed onto buildings, and you'd have buildings that produce their own power!

Color Chameleons

And speaking of changing color, how would you like to change the color of your clothes or your room with the touch of a button? This isn't as farfetched as it sounds. Scientists have already created certain kinds of nanocrystals that change shape when an electric current flows through them. When they change shape, they reflect light differently—and so change the color of the fabric, paint, or other material that contains them.

Imagine wearing a blue shirt to school and changing it to green when you meet your friends to play ball later. Or changing the color of your bedroom walls to match your mood!

Smart Clothing

The world already has electronic fabrics. These are fabrics that are wired—they've got conductive fibers (fibers that transmit electricity) woven into them. Clothing made out of such fabrics is very bulky to wear. But wait until nanotechnology downsizes electronics. Then clothes can be wired for almost anything, from changing color to keeping you cool or warm. They might even have sensors to monitor your temperature and heart rate!

Scientists predict that nanosensors will not just be used for medical purposes in the years to come. Perhaps they'll help keep track of your schoolbooks and keys. Imagine cartons of milk equipped with sensors that tell the store manager when they have been on the shelf too long. Or maybe your favorite pair of jeans will have sensors that tell the washing machine how hot or cold to make the water.

Over the next few years, some of these nanotech predictions will probably become realities. If you haven't felt the impact of nanotechnology in your life yet, it won't be long before you do.

Blending In

The military is very interested in fabrics that change color. Modern soldiers wear camouflage uniforms with patterns printed on them. Imagine clothing that can change color to match a person's background perfectly, no matter what it looks like. In a jungle, your clothes would turn shades of green. If you stood against a brick wall, they'd switch to dark reds to help you blend right in.

chapter 5

Nanobots and Beyond

So far, we've talked about nanotechnology mostly as scientists and engineers building things—putting together atoms and molecules to create new materials, new devices and, eventually, nanomachines. But there is another possibility. It's one that some scientists see happening many years from now. Other scientists don't think it ever will.

What is this long-range nanotech development? The creation of advanced nanomachines called nanobots.

Nanobot is short for nanoscale robot. According to some nanotechnology

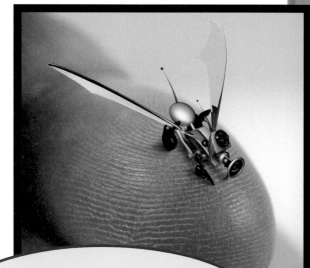

Our current ability to miniaturize machines is still limited to macrosized (visible) devices like this spy fly. But with the rapid advances in nanotechnology, nanobots could be in our future.

Artwork showing theoretical nanobots in a human eye. In the future, we may be able to build nanobots that can enter and treat every part of the body, including complex organs such as eyes, the brain, and the heart.

researchers, nano-bots would be the ultimate nanotools. Once built, they would be programmed to build things on their own. They could assemble atoms and molecules to make just about anything we wanted.

The Bright Side

Wouldn't that be great? Anything you wanted, nanobots could make. Nanobots wouldn't have to use expensive raw materials. They would assemble the right molecules built from atoms that are all around us.

There would be no need to raise cows for milk. Nanobots would just assemble the right molecules to make milk directly. They could also make the glass that you drank it out of. Need some water to rinse out your glass? Nanobots could simply bond hydrogen and oxygen atoms together to make H_2O!

The Dark Side

At first glance, nanobots would seem to be the answer to all our problems. We'd never want for anything. We'd be able to build or fix everything.

But scientists point out that because nanobots would be so small, there would have to be a lot of them. You'd need millions, even billions of them to assemble all the molecules needed to make something as "simple" as a glass of milk. It would be impossible for scientists to build all those nanobots. It would take forever.

An artist's view of a nanobot's possible ability to repair the human body, including DNA (above). Another artist created this image of a nanobot building nanocircuitry. Nanobots and their potential abilities remain only ideas.

So in order for this scheme to work, nanobots programmed to do a specific task would need to do more than assemble molecules to make something. They would first need to assemble molecules to make copies of themselves until there were enough nanobots to do the job. In other words, they would be self-replicating.

FUN FACT!
Does it seem impossible that very small machines could make very large objects? It's not. It's happening all around you right now. It's even happening inside you. Cells are tiny living machines. Cells work together to build big things, from giant oak trees and great blue whales to basketball superstars. Cells also self-replicate each time they divide.

A medical nanobot treats a human fetus in this artwork. Some scientists caution that creating nanomachines that can heal, build, and repair means that they could also be able to harm and destroy.

It's the idea of self-replicating nanobots that alarms some people. What if they got out of control? What if they started replicating and never stopped? And what if . . .

Gray Goo

What if . . . they started taking things apart?

If it's possible to program nanobots to assemble molecules to build things, the opposite could be possible too. Imagine nanobots that were programmed (or malfunctioned) to disassemble matter, that is, to take things apart molecule by molecule.

When Nanobots Attack

Science fiction writer Michael Crichton's book *Prey* is a story based on the idea of nanobots gone wild. In the book, a swarm of self-replicating microscopic machines escapes from a research lab. And like the dinosaurs in Crichton's *Jurassic Park*, the nanobots turn on the scientists who created them.

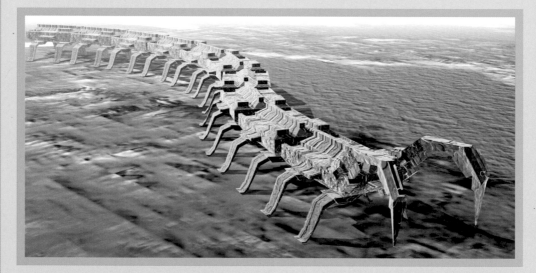

This illustration of nanobots on the march shows people's fear about nanotechnology going bad, turning on its creators and harming instead of helping.

Imagine them replicating to make more disassemblers. Would they start disassembling (taking apart) everything around them? Where would it end? If we couldn't stop them, would they eventually disassemble all matter, leaving nothing behind but a jumble of atoms and molecules, what nanotechnologists call gray goo?

No one really knows. But no one wants to take chances, either. That's why scientists are building in safeguards as nanotechnology progresses. There are regulations about how research is carried out. Some kinds of nanodevices are designed to work only under special laboratory conditions.

At this point, nanobots are still the stuff of science fiction novels. Fundamental questions about them need to be answered. For example, it takes energy to move molecules and bond them together. Where would nanobots get the energy to do this?

Making nanobots would be really difficult. But impossible? That remains to be seen.

Changing Everything

Back in 1959, when Richard Feynman spoke about creating new things on a very small scale, some people smiled and dismissed his ideas as fantasy. But many people did the same thing back in the early 1900s when the Wright brothers were building an airplane. These people found it impossible to believe that flying machines would ever become a reality. Yet in 1903, the Wright brothers got their plane off the ground. Soon planes filled the skies. Then satellites and spaceships flew above the sky and out into space. In 1969, just sixty-seven years after the first successful airplane flight, men landed on the moon! Who could have predicted all those amazing changes would occur in such a relatively short time?

Richard Feynman (*above*) predicted that we could create on a very small scale. Each day, his vision becomes closer to being true in the world of nanotechnology.

Think of the technology that surrounds us. We have cell phones, wireless computers, and virtual reality games. Just a few years ago, these things seemed like impossible fantasies too.

There's no longer any question that nanotechnology is possible. It's happening. It's already begun to change our lives. No one knows exactly where this new technology will lead. But one thing is certain: nanotechnology has the potential to change everything!

Glossary

atomic force microscope (AFM): a microscope that produces an image of atoms and molecules on the surface of an object or material

atoms: the basic building blocks of matter

buckminsterfullerene: a spherical (round) form of carbon composed of sixty carbon atoms. It is also called a fullerene or a buckyball.

carbon nanotubes: a tubelike form of carbon

circuit: the continuous, controlled path of a current of electricity

matter: the material "stuff" that makes up the observable universe

molecules: a small unit of matter composed of a group of atoms bonded together

nanobots: nanometer-sized robots, or nanomachines that are able to build objects by assembling molecules

nanodevices: nanometer-sized structures that carry out specific tasks

nanomaterials: particles, crystals, and other nanometer-sized substances used as building materials in nanotechnology

nanometer: 1 billionth of a meter

nanotechnology: a new scientific field that involves creating things on an ultra-small scale by moving individual atoms and molecules

quantum dots: very small nanocrystals that glow when exposed to ultraviolet light

scanning tunneling microscope (STM): a microscope that uses a tiny probe to produce an image of the atoms on the surface of a piece of metal

self-replicating: able to make copies of oneself

Selected Bibliography

Angelucci, Rocky. "A Beginner's Guide to Nanotechnology." *Dallas Business Journal*, September 10, 2001.

Bellis, Mary. "Scanning Tunneling Microscope." *About.com: Inventors*. N.d. http://inventors.about.com/library/inventors/blstm.htm?terms=Gerd+Binnig (July 2004).

"Buckyballs." *National Science Foundation.* April 1, 2000. http://www.nsf.gov/od/lpa/nsf50/nsfoutreach/htm/n50_z2/pages_z3/08_pg.htm (July 2004).

Drexler, Eric. "Engines of Creation." *Foresight Institute.* April 1996. http://www.foresight.org/EOC/index.html (July 2004).

Freitas, Robert A. "Say 'AH!'" *Sciences*, July/August 2000.

Harris, Peter J. F. "A Carbon Nanotube Page." N.d. http://www.personal.rdg.ac.uk/%7Escsharip/tubes.htm (June 2004).

"Nanotechnology." *National Science Foundation Office of Legislative and Public Affairs.* April 2003. http://www.nsf.gov/od/lpa/news/03/fsnano_03.htm (July 2004).

"Nanotechnology Introduction." *Nanotechnology Now*. N.d. http://www.nanotech-now.com/introduction.htm (August 2004).

Roston, Eric. "Very Small Business." *Time*. September 23, 2002. http://www.time.com/time/archive/printout/0,23657,1003306,00.html (May 2005).

Scientific American. *Understanding Nanotechnology*. New York: Warner Books, 2002.

Uldrich, Jack, and Deb Newberry. *The Next Big Thing Is Really Small*. New York: Crown Business, 2003.

Venere, Emil. "Nanotechnology: What Is It?" *Purdue News*. September 7, 2001. http://news.uns.purdue.edu/UNS/html4ever/010907.Nanotech.whatisit.html (July 2004).

Further Reading and Websites

Darling, David. *Micromachines and Nanotechnology: The Amazing New World of the Ultrasmall*. South Orange, NJ: Dillon Press, 1995.

This book presents an overview of the technology behind making ultrasmall devices. The author discusses microelectronics, micromachines, and nanotechnology.

Foresight Institute

http://www.foresight.org

Explore the writings of some of nanotechnology's founders at the institute's website.

Maddox, Diane. *Nanotechnology*. San Diego: Blackbirch Press, 2005.

Maddox covers the basics of the emerging field of nanotechnology and its applications.

Nanokids

http://nanokids.rice.edu/

After being introduced to the nanoscale world, visitors can join the NanoScholars Club to become part of a science research team.

Nanotech Now

http://www.nanotech-now.com/nanotube-buckyball-sites.htm

Check out carbon nanotubes and buckyballs and see 3-D pictures of these structures.

The National Nanotechnology Initiative

http://www.nano.gov.

The NNI's website provides nanotech news, facts, applications, and an education center.

Science Central News

http://www.sciencecentral.com

Search this site for the latest news reports about breakthroughs in nanotechnology.

Index

Photo Acknowledgments

The images in this book are used with the permission of: William Johnston/courtesy of Ernest Orlando Lawrence Berkeley National Laboratory Image Library, background image on p. 1 and even pages; © Todd Strand/Independent Picture Service, pp. 5, 20 (top and middle), 21 (all); © SuperStock Inc./SuperStock, pp. 7, 20 (bottom); © age fotostock/SuperStock, p. 8; © George Musil/Visuals Unlimited, p. 9; © IBMRL/Visuals Unlimited, p. 10 (all); © Ed Kashi/CORBIS, p. 11; © Graham J. Hills/Photo Researchers, Inc., p. 12; © Michael L. Abramson/Time Life Pictures/Getty Images, p. 13; courtesy of International Business Machines Corporation. Unauthorized use not permitted, p. 14; © Geoff Tompkinson/Photo Researchers, Inc., p. 15 (both); © Delft University of Technology/Photo Researchers, Inc., p. 16; Sgt. Lorie Jewell/courtesy of U.S. Army, p. 19 (both); SUNCLEAN glass photo courtesy PPG Industries, Inc., p. 22 (all); © Digital Art/CORBIS, pp. 23, 36; © John Springer Collection/CORBIS, p. 25; courtesy of Diane S. Lidke, PhD., Max Planck Institute for Biophysical Chemistry, p. 26; © David McCarthy/Photo Researchers, Inc., p. 27; courtesy of YinYin Guo, Forrest Blocker and Peixuan Guo, Purdue University, p. 29; © Franz Himpsel/University of Wisconsin/Photo Researchers, Inc., p. 31 (both); © STR/AFP/Getty Images, p. 32; NASA Marshall Space Flight Center, p. 33; © Take 27 Ltd./Photo Researchers, Inc., p. 37 (all); © Victor Habbick Visions/Photo Researchers, Inc., p. 38 (both); © Christian Darkin/Photo Researchers, Inc., pp. 39, 40; courtesy of the Archives, California Institute of Technology. Photograph of Richard Feynman used by permission of Melanie Jackson Agency, L.L.C., p. 41.

Front cover: William Johnston/courtesy of Ernest Orlando Lawrence Berkeley National Laboratory Image Library, background; © Ghim Wei Ho and Professor Mark Welland, Nanostructure Center, University of Cambridge (top and bottom left); Lawrence Berkeley National Laboratory/Department of Energy Photo Library (bottom center); © Digital Art/CORBIS (bottom right). Back cover: William Johnston/courtesy of Ernest Orlando Lawrence Berkeley National Laboratory Image Library, background.

About the Author

Rebecca L. Johnson, a South Dakota native, has written more than fifty books for children and young adults. Among her recent titles is a series about water biomes (A Journey into the Ocean/a River/a Lake/an Estuary/a Wetland) that received the Society of School Librarians International Best Book of 2004 award for science K–6. In addition to writing books, Johnson also works part-time as a writer for the U.S. Geological Survey's National Center for Earth Resources Observation and Science (EROS), a science research center that specializes in using satellite images to learn more about the earth.